MIGHTY MEN OF VALOR: BOOK 1

Strength

PRIORITIES FOR KINGDOM LIVING

RYAN,

"Be strong..."
JOSHUA 1:6,7,9

BLESSINGS,
MIKE + DONNETTE
MARTIN

mike@makeamark.net

MIGHTY MEN OF VALOR: BOOK 1

Strength

PRIORITIES FOR KINGDOM LIVING

Dean Ridings | Bob Jones | Scott Ballenger

Make a Mark
MINISTRIES

6660 Delmonico Drive, Suite D-140 • Colorado Springs, Colorado 80919

E-mail info@makeamark.net • Web www.makeamark.net
www.facebook.com/makeamarkministries

Mighty Men of Valor: Book 1

Strength

PRIORITIES FOR KINGDOM LIVING

_____

Mighty Man of Valor's Name

_____
_____
_____
_____
_____
_____
_____

Name and Contact Information of Warrior Brother(s)

_____

Date Started

_____

Date Completed

As iron sharpens iron,
so one man sharpens another.
Proverbs 27:17

Mighty Men of Valor: Book 1 – Strength

A Make a Mark Ministries Bible Study
Copyright © 2013 by Dean Ridings, Bob Jones, Scott Ballenger

This is the first in the series of Priorities for Kingdom Living, which includes:

Mighty Men of Valor: Book 2 – Courage
Mighty Men of Valor: Book 3 – Passion

Design: Steve Learned

Cover Photo: ©iStockphoto.com/Nature247

Contents

Introduction

"The Lord is with you, you mighty man of valor!" (Judges 6:12, NKJV). As the angel of the Lord greeted Gideon in Old Testament times, so we welcome you to an adventure in becoming one of God's choice warriors.

Why warriors? Because since the Garden of Eden we have three enemies seeking to usurp God's rule over His creation: the world (temptations around us), the flesh (our own evil desires), and the devil (yes, the Bible says he's real and deadly). Thus, we have an enemy within and enemies without, all waging constant battle against us.

To fight these enemies, we need *strength*, the kind that comes from God alone! Time and again in Scripture, God calls His men to be strong. Gideon and others who served God at a time when everyone was doing what seemed right in their own eyes, David and his armies that followed him, and Christian men in New Testament times are charged with standing strong. Men of valor need great strength.

So, does this mean that we need to join a gym, buy a weight set, or get into bodybuilding? No, God has a different strength in mind. When faced with defeat and the loss of his family and friends, "David found strength in the Lord his God" (1 Samuel 30:6). Paul urged the Ephesians to "be strong in the Lord and in his mighty power" (Ephesians 6:10).

You see, God is not necessarily calling men to lift weights but broken spirits before Him, not so much to build bulging biceps but to love and build up one another in Christ. Our concern should be less with winning strongman competitions than it is with winning others to the kingdom of God.

We commend the exercises in this Bible study to help you develop your spiritual "muscles." The Mighty Men of Valor we see in Scripture and walking among us today have three distinct characteristics: They are men of *strength, courage, and passion.* In this Bible study we unpack the first characteristic, strength. In follow-up studies we look at courage and passion.

As you go through this study, we hope you will become more and more the mighty warrior God sees you as and is developing you to be. Our prayer is that you would join the ranks of men committed to be Mighty Men of Valor who passionately live for good and for God in this generation—building others who will passionately live for Jesus in the next!

Using this Study

As with the additional Bible studies in this series—*Mighty Men of Valor: Book 2 - Courage* and *Mighty Men of Valor: Book 3 - Passion*—this study can be used in three essential ways.

First, you can use it as a daily devotional. We strongly encourage every man to take time out for a daily meeting—or *appointment*—with God. Make it a time of talking to God, looking into His Word, and asking Him to help you apply it to your life today.

Notice how Jesus, our example for life and ministry, made this a priority in His life. "Very early in the morning, while it was still dark, Jesus got up, left the house and went off to a solitary place, where he prayed" (Mark 1:35).

A second way you can use this study is to connect with other men—in the spirit of Hebrews 10:24-25—to spur one another on toward becoming Mighty Men of Valor. You may think of this as walking "Side-by-Side," meeting weekly for mutual growth, mutual support, and mutual accountability.

More than merely going through the Bible study together, it's all about helping one another "contend for the faith that was once for all entrusted to the saints" (see Jude 3) in the midst of 21st century reality.

"Warrior Brothers" may be traditional mentoring or discipleship relationships between "mature" and their protégé "young" disciples, such as Elijah and Elisha or Paul and Timothy. Or they may be mutual discipleship or peer co-mentoring relationships between any two believers—no matter where they are in their faith—such as David and Jonathan or Paul and Barnabas. King Solomon puts it this way: "As iron sharpens iron, so one man sharpens another" (Proverbs 27:17).

Finally, a third way to use this study is in a triad or small-group setting. Think of Jesus, once again. He focused on a small group of men (see Luke 6:13-16). He built into their lives, strategically moving them along the discipleship journey. Yes, at times He fed thousands with physical and spiritual food; mainly, though, He invested in the Twelve.

If you're a man looking to make a key investment in other men, consider starting a small group. You might pray to have such an influence on a dozen lives. If you meet or exceed that goal, consider asking God ultimately to use you to invest in the lives of 300 men—like the small band that formed Gideon's army!

However you use this tool, remember that you are not alone. Along the way Jesus will both *guide* and *grow* you toward greater godliness (see Romans 8:28-29; Philippians 1:6; 2 Corinthians 3:18). Indeed, the Lord is with you, Mighty Man of Valor!

New Life
Turning Toward God

*"Being a Christian is more than just an
instantaneous conversion—it is a daily process whereby
you grow to be more and more like Christ."*
—Billy Graham

Read & Reflect

Read and reflect on Matthew 9:9-13. Consider the following
question: *How good do you have to be for God to look upon you
with favor—for Jesus to ask you to follow Him?*

_____

_____

_____

_____

The Challenge

Matthew was used to scorn and rejection from the Jews, espe-
cially the Jewish leaders. As a tax gatherer, he worked for the
Roman conquerors and got rich by gouging his countrymen. He
was everything a pious Jew despised—dishonest, a traitor to his
country—and he hung out with thugs and prostitutes: not at the
top of anyone's list to have as a friend. Not anyone except Jesus,
that is.

When Jesus passed Matthew's tax table, He looked with compassion at the hated tax gatherer and simply called out, "Follow
me." Matthew was blown away! Here was a Rabbi, a godly man,
calling *him*, the outcast, to be part of His team. Not only did

Matthew get up and follow Jesus, but he called all his friends, the other so-called dregs of Jewish society, and threw a party with Jesus and His disciples as guests of honor. And there was Jesus, seemingly at home with this group of sinners.

This was too much for the Jewish leaders. It was an outrage! They indignantly asked, "Why does your teacher eat with tax collectors and sinners?" Such people were deemed not good enough for God to give them any notice. Any *righteous* Jew would know this. But Jesus, quoting Hosea 6:6, which the leaders well knew, responded, "'I desire mercy, not sacrifice.' For I have not come to call the righteous, but sinners." Jesus called the worst sinners of His day to be His followers. He still does the same today.

Living It Out

God has no grandchildren, only children, and the only way to become God's child is to believe in His Son, Jesus Christ, for the forgiveness of sins. Franklin Graham, son of renowned evangelist Billy Graham, learned early on that not even the name "Graham" is a free pass into heaven.

Born in 1952 in Ashville, North Carolina, Franklin was the fourth of five children. Though he grew up in a home that honored God, Franklin didn't. He went to a Christian high school and dropped out in his junior year, requiring him to finish later. In college he masterminded a shower prank gone awry that eventually flooded an entire building. He was a self-described "rebellious, beer-drinking motorcyclist."

Then, at age 22, Franklin found himself in a hotel room on his knees before God, as Jesus' words pierced his heart: "I am the way and the truth and the life. No one comes to the Father except through me" (John 14:6). Here's how Franklin puts it today: "Am I ready to stand before a Holy God? What will it take? People say, 'Oh, if I'm good, God will take me [to heaven] or if I give to good causes, I'll go.' But that's not what the Bible teaches."

Franklin now serves as president and CEO of Samaritan's Purse, which seeks to touch people in Jesus' name by meeting the needs of the poor, sick, and suffering in more than 100 countries. He also heads the Billy Graham Evangelistic Association, and has led crusades around the world. Though Franklin continues to take heat for publicly praying in Jesus' name and speaking against false religion, he's uncompromising on his mission to "unabashedly seek souls" with the clarion call, "Jesus is the only way."

→ What would it take for you to follow Jesus, wholly and completely?

_____

_____

_____

_____

→ Matthew threw a party and invited all of his "cruddy buddies." What would it look like for you to share the hope that you have with your friends who don't yet know Jesus (see 1 Peter 3:15)?

_____

_____

_____

_____

→ What might living a life with the motto "Jesus is the only way" look like for you? What would the implications be?

_____

_____

Takeaway Truth

Some of the greatest joys of being a Christian are discovering "how wide and long and high and deep is the love of Christ" (Ephesians 3:18), and then realizing that He's made you an ambassador of this great love to the world around you. He can use a man like you to help others find new life in Christ. A life of meaning and purpose is founded on God's great love for you through Jesus Christ and your response in a personal relationship with Him. You have an opportunity to tell others about the very real changes He has brought to your life. Now go and live today as a man called to follow Christ and to proclaim the Good News of His love to others!

Valor Prayer

ALMIGHTY GOD, You are so good and gracious to take personal notice of me. As I put my name into John 3:16, I realize that You loved me so much that You sent Your only Son to die on the cross for me, and that if I believe in Jesus I will not live eternally apart from You but have life beyond this life with You. May I not only know this in my heart but live it out today. This is what You mean by Your present-day invitation: "Follow Me." As I follow, please use me to help others find new life in Jesus Christ, the only way!

For Further Investigation

→ Romans 5:6-11
→ Ephesians 4:11-15
→ Philippians 2:12-13

God's Word

Hearing from God

> *"The Bible is the inevitable*
> *outcome of God's continuous speech. It is the*
> *infallible declaration of His mind."*
> **—A. W. Tozer**

Read & Reflect

Read and reflect on 2 Timothy 3:1-17. Consider the following
question: *How can I stay anchored and grow in my faith amid the
pressures and temptations of our world?*

_____

_____

_____

_____

The Challenge

What an incredible ministry the apostle Paul had! Near the end
when he was sitting in prison awaiting execution, his thoughts
turned to his young disciple Timothy. Timothy was in Ephesus,
a large, cosmopolitan city where religions abounded and false
teachers prospered. So Paul, longing to encourage his friend
before he himself went to be with the Lord, sent a letter outlining
the most important priorities for a follower of Christ in such a
situation.

Always a realist, Paul described the evil of putting oneself above
God and His kingdom and the persecution of Christians that fol-
lows. There was such a pressure on a follower of Christ to compro-

mise with the pleasures of the world! How could one stand strong, even grow closer to the Lord in the midst of such temptation?

Among his counsel, Paul charged Timothy to be steeped in God's Word. Only the Scriptures can make a person "wise for salvation" even at an early age (2 Timothy 3:15). Only God's Word, the Bible, is literally *breathed out* by God Himself (2 Timothy 3:16). Only His Word gives wisdom for life, for ministry, for growing toward greater godliness. By continuing to read, study and practice the Word of God, Timothy would be equipped to face the challenges of his world long after Paul was no longer here on earth. God used the Gospel in the lives of saints of old—and He has done so through the generations and for His people today.

Living It Out

Few took notice of William Tyndale's birth in North Nibley, England, in 1494. Some 40 years later, more looked on as he was arrested and imprisoned for heresy and treason. His crime? Translating the New Testament into English. For that Tyndale was first strangled, and then burned at the stake. As to his legacy, his life and ministry have positively affected countless individuals through the years and to this very day.

Tyndale attended Oxford and Cambridge and received his Master's at age 21. The theologian and scholar was a gifted linguist who spoke eight languages, being proficient in ancient Hebrew and Greek. He found his passion and purpose when Erasmus's words leaped off the page: "Christ desires His mysteries to be published abroad as widely as possible. I would that [the Gospels and the epistles of Paul] were translated into all languages, of all Christian people, and that they might be read and known."

When Tyndale produced the first English New Testament, authorities bought up all copies—inadvertently financing a more refined subsequent edition. A Roman Catholic clergyman took issue, saying, "We are better to be without God's laws than the

Pope's." Tyndale fired back, "If God spare my life ere many years, I will cause the boy that drives the plow to know more of the Scriptures than you!"

People through the years have sought to silence God's truth, including those who nailed Jesus to the cross. Agents of the king and the Anglican Church sought to silence God's servant Tyndale, yet only a year after his death came the release of the complete English language Bible translated directly from the original languages, the "Matthew–Tyndale Bible." Today Bible distribution is estimated in the billions, with an average of four English editions readily available in American homes.

→ Who's a man you know that trusts God and takes Him at His word? Let his walk encourage you that such a life can be lived!

_____

_____

_____

_____

→ How does it encourage you to know that the Bible is "God breathed," that it's not merely words about God but it's _the Word of God?_

_____

_____

_____

_____

→ What does it look like to get into God's Word daily, to read, study, and chew on it so that it becomes more natural to put it into practice?

_____

_____

_____

_____

Takeaway Truth

God's Word is perfect. Yes, it's tough to live as a Christ-follower in this world; it takes great strength to walk the narrow path of righteousness. Where do we find strength and guidance to do so? God has given us wisdom in His perfect manuscript to us, the Bible. Reading, learning, memorizing, and meditating on His Word is the key to understanding how He would have us react to the world and live our lives. Grab another man and talk about it, just as iron sharpens iron. Now go and live today seeking His kingdom and His righteousness through His Word so that you will live the life He intends for you!

Valor Prayer

HEAVENLY FATHER, thank You for the Bible. Give me the strength and courage to live by it, even to die for it if it comes to that. Thank You that it's "God breathed," that You spoke to and through the various authors to give us a consistent message of Your love, grace, compassion, and wisdom—everything I need for life and godliness, as You say in 2 Peter 1:3. I'm grateful as well that it's readily available. Lord, may Your Word live in me and guide me as I seek not merely to listen to it but to do what it says (James 1:22)!

For Further Investigation

→ Psalm 19:7-11
→ Psalm 119 (pick any verse!)
→ Hebrews 4:12

Prayer
Talking with God

"Prayer breaks all bars, dissolves all chains,
opens all prisons, and widens all straits by which
God's saints have been held."
—E. M. Bounds

Read & Reflect

Read and reflect on Daniel 6:1-28. Consider the following question: *How does prayer affect my walk with God?*

_____

_____

_____

_____

The Challenge

The advisers to King Darius were frustrated beyond endurance! Jealous of Daniel's success, they sought to discredit him before the king. But they could not find anything of which to accuse him, because "an excellent spirit was in him" (ESV). No financial misdealings, no moral failures, no slick political schemes behind the scenes. How could they bring Daniel down and raise themselves up in the king's eyes? That's when it hit them. They knew Daniel prayed to God every day, even though the king wanted people to worship him.

So they tricked the king into signing a law making it illegal to pray to any god but himself for 30 days. What would Daniel do? He could either give up his time with God for a month, or he could face death by lions. As soon as the king signed the law, Daniel, ever faithful to God, went home to pray. And he continued to talk with God just as always. As a result, he was arrested and thrown to the lions. But, miraculously, God delivered him. The king actually threw the dishonest advisers into the same lion den!

Daniel was faithful to pray. And how did this affect his walk with God? God Himself was glorified as the king proclaimed that everyone in his kingdom was to "fear and reverence the God of Daniel." Daniel not only was rescued from the lions, but he "prospered during the reign of Darius and the reign of Cyrus the Persian." Daniel trusted God and talked with Him daily, and God blessed him. God is looking for men of spiritual strength to do so today.

Living It Out

George Müller was a humble, God-fearing man who lived in the nineteenth century and longed to serve the Lord with his all. He sought to know God through His Word, help other people know and trust Him, and make a kingdom difference where he lived in Bristol, England. But how? George prayed persistently for clear direction, and God gripped his heart with the plight of the orphan.

With a vision from God and what amounted to about a half dollar in his pocket, he sought provision from the Lord for the work to which he'd been called. What's more, he was committed to expressing his needs to no man, only God. What began with two shillings became some £1,500,000 ($7.5 million), most of which he used to build and care for the orphanage of five buildings covering 13 acres on Ashley Downs that 2,000 children at a time would call home.

His prayers were practical: for men who would work through the night to fix a boiler and the weather to let up; for divine direction to identify a drain blockage; for a constant provision of food for the children. His perspective was, "If the Lord fails me at this time, it will be the first time."

George made every need known to God, and more than 100,000 children passed through the orphanage in his lifetime. He was the father of orphans, a prayer warrior, a modest man who described his legacy this way: "George Müller, nothing. The Lord Jesus, everything. In himself worse than nothing. By grace, in Christ, the son of the King."

→ Who's the greatest person of prayer that you know? What is it about his or her life that stands out?

_____

_____

_____

_____

→ How have you seen prayer make a difference, either in your own life or in someone else's?

_____

_____

_____

_____

→ The acronym PUSH—Pray Until Something Happens—reminds us to be steadfast in prayer. What might it look like for you to take the next step toward becoming a persistent prayer warrior?

_____

_____

_____

_____

Takeaway Truth

God wants to talk with you. He desires to be connected to you constantly through prayer and guide you in a powerful way to live a godly life in a broken world. You are His creation, in whom He has planted dreams, hopes, and spiritual gifts to fulfill His plan. He will give you the desires of your heart as He glorifies Himself through your life. Now go and live today unashamed to pray for a life that glorifies Him and prepare to be amazed at how He will respond!

Valor Prayer

HEAVENLY FATHER, as I look back on my life, I can see how You have been there and responded to prayer. You've answered "yes," "no," "wait awhile," but You've always answered. Forgive me for the many times I've tried to do things on my own rather than talk to and trust wholly and completely in You. Help me to grow to become a persistent prayer warrior who worships and adores You, confesses sin before You, casts my cares upon You, and never fails to give thanks . . . most of all for Jesus my Savior and Lord!

For Further Investigation

→ Psalm 108:1-6
→ Matthew 7:7-11
→ James 5:13-16

Warfare
Engaging the Battle

"There is no neutral ground in the universe;
every square inch, every split second is claimed by God
and counterclaimed by Satan."
—C. S. Lewis

Read & Reflect

Read and reflect on Luke 4:1-13. Consider the following question:
How can I successfully battle the temptations of the enemy?

_____

_____

_____

_____

The Challenge

Jesus had just been baptized, the Holy Spirit descended on Him
like a dove, and the Father's voice echoed among the crowd and
in Jesus' ears: "You are my Son, whom I love; with you I am well
pleased" (Luke 3:22). Soon afterward God's old adversary—Satan,
also called the devil, who led a rebellion in heaven that still affects
us today—arrived to try to trip Jesus up at the start of His ministry. If ever there was a ripe moment for the devil to derail God's
rescue mission to seek and save the lost, this was it.

Satan tempted Jesus to use His power for selfish needs. He
tried to get Jesus to take a short cut away from the cross, God's
plan to save us from Satan's stronghold when we all chose to sin.
The devil urged Jesus to make a public display of His power by

throwing Himself off the top of the temple. Jesus was tired, hungry and vulnerable in His humanity to the strongest temptations that the enemy could throw at Him. Yet even in this condition, Jesus successfully defeated the enemy. Satan was frustrated again! But how?

Jesus turned to God's words in the book of Deuteronomy to thwart the enemy's three temptations. Even from His youth, Jesus had memorized and internalized the Scriptures. He understood their meaning, and so was able to apply them to the specific tests of Satan. Jesus knew that God's truth always trumps the devil's lies. As the light pierces the darkness, God's Word vanquishes the enemy in our lives as well.

Living It Out

Martin Luther was born in 1483 to middle-class peasant laborers in the small town of Eisleben, Germany. By age 21, his parents' sacrifice to provide him a decent education had paid off: Martin had a Master of Arts degree from the University of Erfurt, where he continued his studies toward fulfilling his father's dream for him of becoming a lawyer. Then came the thunderstorm, which changed everything. Martin was on horseback when a thunderbolt struck so close that he feared for his life and his eternal soul. Without thinking, he cried out a vow to become a monk if God spared his life. To his parents' dismay, Martin stopped his studies, sold his books, and entered the monastery.

It was the Bible, the Word of God, that helped him overcome his lingering fears of death and eternal judgment. Like a beam of sun through a storm, Martin was struck by the assurance that a person is saved by grace through faith (see Ephesians 2:8-9). The Bible became his daily bread, and he relied on it as he wrote and posted his now well-known "95 Theses" to correct errors in the church of his day. He even translated the New Testament into German, so "common people" could read it for themselves.

Still, being troubled by the devil proved a constant theme in Martin's life. It was God's Word that convinced him the enemy was a defeated foe, like a chained dog. "Why should you fear, why should you be afraid?" he wrote. "Do you not know that the prince of this world has been judged? He is no lord, no prince any more. You have a different, a stronger Lord, Christ, who has overcome and bound him." Cling to God's Word and pray regularly—that's his bottom line on how to stand firm amid a very real spiritual battle.

→ When you were growing up, or perhaps even before this particular lesson, what did you think of when people said "the devil" or "Satan" (e.g., a guy with horns wearing a red suit)?

_____

_____

_____

_____

→ Think about how Jesus described His mission here on earth, to seek and save what was lost (Luke 19:10). In light of this lesson, what do you think was "lost" and how did it happen?

_____

_____

_____

_____

→ Martin Luther saw Satan and his fallen-angel followers as defeated foes because of the finished work of Jesus, "triumphing over them by the cross" (Colossians 2:15). How does this encourage you today?

_____

_____

_____

_____

Takeaway Truth

God is with you in the battle. Yes, you are in enemy-occupied territory. Yet never forget that the Father has equipped you with allies in the battle. He has given you His Son, Jesus, and hope in His resurrection; the Holy Spirit dwelling within you as your counselor and guide; the truth of Scripture to defeat demonic lies; the full armor of God; and a band of brothers in the body of Christ. Now go and live today, understanding your allies and adversary, and engaging in the battle to make a difference for eternity!

Valor Prayer

HEAVENLY FATHER, Mighty Warrior and Champion, thank You for sending Your Son, Jesus, to seek and save what was lost—like me. The Bible tells me that Satan is a roaring lion seeking someone to devour (1 Peter 5:8), and I need only to look around me—as well as at my own journey—to see how this enemy has taken a toll. Right here, right now, I declare afresh my trust and hope in You to keep this defeated foe far from me and those around me. Use me to help others find freedom from the enemy. Commissioned by Jesus (Matthew 28:18-20) and empowered by the Holy Spirit (Acts 1:8), may I be a Mighty Man of Valor used of You today to help fulfill that great mission to seek and save what was lost.

For Further Investigation

→ John 10:1-18
→ Ephesians 6:10-18
→ James 4:7-10

Purity
Pursuing Righteousness

"Resolved, never to do anything
which I would be afraid to do if it were
the last hour of my life."
—Jonathan Edwards

Read & Reflect

Read and reflect on Genesis 39:6-20. Consider the following
question: *What does a man gain by resisting sexual temptation?*

_____

_____

_____

_____

The Challenge

Joseph was a young man in the prime of life. Sold into slavery by
his brothers, Joseph became the chief overseer in the house of
Potiphar, an Egyptian officer. The young Hebrew was a master
manager, honest, capable and successful in whatever he did. Not
only was he a gifted overseer, he was also a handsome, virile man,
and he attracted the eye of the master's wife. One day, she bra-
zenly offered herself to him, but he refused to violate the trust of
his master or his God.

Frustrated by his refusal, she persisted. For days she tried to
seduce him, until one day she caught him in the house alone.
She grabbed his cloak and demanded his sexual attentions. Like
a scene out of an R-rated movie, Joseph was faced with a choice.

But unlike many movie scenes, his eyes were on the Lord, not the woman. Joseph left his cloak in her hands and ran away. Angry at his rejection, she falsely accused of him attempting to rape her, and Joseph was thrown into prison.

Wait a minute! Joseph obeyed God and remained sexually pure. And for that, he was thrown into prison? Keep reading: "the Lord was with him; he showed him kindness and granted him favor in the eyes of the prison warden. So the warden put Joseph in charge of all those held in the prison, and he was made responsible for all that was done there" (Genesis 39:21-22).

Joseph gained the favor of both God and man, a clear conscience, a deep satisfaction in the power of God at work within him, and the trust of everyone who came into contact with him. Ultimately, Joseph gained a position of great responsibility as second in command of the greatest country in that world, where he was able to save his family and the Egyptian nation from starvation. God honored Joseph for his faithfulness and obedience. He does the same today.

Living It Out

Bob Harrington was known as The Chaplain of Bourbon Street, one of the most popular preachers in the United States. He of all people knew what the Bible taught about self-control, about not giving the devil an inch because he would never be satisfied until he had a mile. He'd seen it happen with too many men, falling into one sin or another.

Then this New Orleans man gave the devil an inch . . . and turned his back on God and family to pursue 19 years of "prodigal living." In the process, he learned just what it means that Christians have an enemy who is relentless in his pursuit to "steal and kill and destroy" (John 10:10).

As the twentieth century drew to a close, just as in Jesus' story of the Prodigal Son, Bob Harrington awoke, came to his senses, and returned to Christ. While he suffered sin's consequences, he was forgiven by God, family, and friends. Bob's experience gave him a surprising platform from which to address other prodigals, resulting in hundreds of men and women coming "home" to Christ.

→ Have you ever felt like a prisoner to your appetite for lust? Where are you in the fight for freedom?

_____

_____

_____

_____

→ How can you remain pure amid *the world, the flesh, and the devil* working against you?

_____

_____

_____

_____

→ Who can help hold you accountable in the area of moral purity? Consider giving him a call, or going out for a meal or coffee to talk more.

_____

_____

_____

_____

_____

Takeaway Truth

God is enough. He is able to satisfy your desires and forgive your transgressions. We all start equally in a place of sin before we turn to God. The truly great news of the Gospel message is that He then sees us as sinless through the redemptive work of our Lord and Savior, Jesus Christ. God continues to sanctify us, to grow us toward greater godliness, until we join Him in heaven. We are to join Him in this work by making purity our aim during our time on earth. Now go and live today as a man who has been purchased with the precious blood of Christ, glorifying your Lord with a life dedicated to Him!

Valor Prayer

HOLY GOD, I live in a world where sexual purity is not easy. Help me to make wise decisions about what I will view, what I will read, what I will think about. You are a strong tower to protect me from my enemy, the devil. Guard my heart as I absorb Your Word into my mind. Give me some brothers in Christ who will keep me on track with Your holiness and purity. Thank You for delivering me from the power of sin in Christ.

For Further Investigation

→ Job 31:1
→ 2 Samuel 11:1-5
→ 1 Thessalonians 4:3-8

PRIORITY 6

Grace

Embracing God's Favor

*"Grace is not only undeserved favor,
but it is favor, shown to the one who has
deserved the very opposite."*
—Harry Ironside

Read & Reflect

Read and reflect on 1 Timothy 1:12-17. Consider the following
question: *How can a man take a total U-turn in life, from Sin City
to the Heavenly Heights?*

_____

_____

_____

_____

The Challenge

Young Timothy needed a shot in the arm. Pastoring the church at
Ephesus was a tough calling, and Tim was getting a bit discouraged. So his old mentor, Paul, wrote him a couple of letters to lift
his spirits. Paul reminded his friend that God's grace was enough
to meet all of life's challenges, and the best way to remember that
was to reflect on Paul's own first encounter with the grace that is
found in Christ alone (find this story in Acts 9).

As a brilliant and deeply committed Pharisee, Paul had persecut-
ed Christians wherever he found them. He would imprison them
and encourage the death penalty for such "traitors" to the Jewish
faith. His hatred for Christians was well known throughout Israel.

But an incredible thing happened to Paul on his way to throw more Christians in jail. He described it this way, "The grace of our Lord was poured out on me abundantly, along with the faith and love that are in Christ Jesus" (1 Timothy 1:14). Paul was blown away! God, acting purely out of grace, reached into his life, forgave his sins, and entrusted him with bringing the Gospel to the Gentiles.

This "Pharisee of Pharisees" was now the "Apostle to the Gentiles." As God's chosen spokesman, Paul endured persecution, hardship, ridicule, and all manner of difficulties for the sake of Christ. God's grace, His unmerited favor, motivated Paul to live for Christ at any cost. When we embrace the grace that God poured out on us in Christ, we enjoy that same motivation.

Living It Out

Brennan Manning was born and raised in Depression-era New York City. He served as a Marine, fought in Korea, and returned home to the States with a hunger to know the God he had heard about as a child. That led Brennan to seminary in Loretto, Pennsylvania, and to a life-changing event that occurred one day when minutes turned into hours as he prayed before a cross.

"Without warning I felt a grip, a hand gripped my heart," Brennan remembers. "I could barely breathe. The awareness of being loved unconditionally was no longer gentle, tender, and comfortable. The love of Christ, the crucified Son of God, for me, took on the wildness, the passion, and the fury of a sudden storm in springtime."

Afterward, Brennan was impassioned to go deeper with God and wholeheartedly serve Him. Through the years, that's led him to do so as a priest, preacher, protector of the poor, prisoner when he stood for justice, and prolific author of such books as *The Ragamuffin Gospel* and *Abba's Child*.

But in the midst of it all, something happened that helped Brennan grasp the grace of God like never before. In the mid-1970s while in a campus ministry in Ft. Lauderdale, the slippery slope of alcohol sidelined him for six months. Through it all he learned a lot about God's grace. "God loves you as you are," he'd often say, "but too much to leave you there."

Since then, through lectures and books—including his latest, *All Is Grace*—his passion is to help people replace the "duty-oriented" Gospel of Law with Jesus' life-transforming Gospel of Grace. "The gospel declares that no matter how dutiful or prayerful we are, we can't save ourselves. What Jesus did was sufficient."

➔ Grace is called "unmerited favor" because it's neither earned nor deserved. It's a gift from God. In "Amazing Grace," it's what "saved a wretch like me." Can you relate? How so?

_____

_____

_____

_____

➔ How would you describe the difference between a "duty-oriented" Gospel of Law and Jesus' life-transforming Gospel of Grace? (See Paul's story in 1 Corinthians 15:1-10.)

_____

_____

_____

➔ Is God's grace "enough" to help you meet all of the challenges you face today or may face in the future? Why is that so?

_____

_____

Takeaway Truth

God's grace is sufficient. The death of Jesus settled the debt for your sins. There is nothing you can do—outside of receiving Jesus Christ as your Lord and Savior—to bridge the gap your sin has created between you and God. The Good News is that there is nothing else you need to do! Doesn't that prompt praise? Indeed, yesterday is behind you; today is the day the Lord has made; let us rejoice and be glad (Psalm 118:24)! We have much to be thankful for, and much to do with our remaining time here on earth. Now go and live today as a man on a mission from God: "Freely you have received, freely give" (Matthew 10:8b)!

Valor Prayer

HEAVENLY FATHER, as I think about the lives of Paul, Brennan Manning, and other faithful Christ-followers, I can't help but think of my own life. Thank You for giving me grace upon grace—not giving me the punishment my sins deserve, but giving me grace beyond measure that I don't deserve. Yet with open hands I offer You myself afresh and accept from You the favor and kindness, forgiveness and love that You freely extend to me. Help me not to take Your grace or You for granted ever again.

For Further Investigation

→ Romans 3:20-24
→ 2 Corinthians 12:8-9
→ Hebrews 4:16

Forgiveness
Dealing with the Past

*"If you don't release
those who have hurt you, you will
begin to resemble them."*
—**Rick Warren**

Read & Reflect

Read and reflect on Matthew 18:21-35. Consider the following
question: *What does authentic forgiveness look like?*

_____

_____

_____

_____

The Challenge

Peter thought he was being generous. The Talmud, a commentary
on Jewish law, only required a man to forgive an offender three
times. Now here is Peter, offering to forgive someone seven times.
But Jesus quickly punctured his bubble: "I tell you, not seven
times, but seventy-seven times." The Lord's point was not about
numbers; He was actually saying that we need to forgive as many
times as we are offended, period. Peter must have stood there in
open-mouthed shock! And the Lord immediately gave Peter a
picture of what forgiveness looks like.

The story is about a servant who owed his king, in today's
money, about what a star professional athlete makes in a career.
Facing a life of slavery because of his debt, the servant begged the

king for patience and a payment plan. Moved with compassion, the king "released him and forgave him the debt." The king gave up his just repayment. Wow! That's like Bank of America telling you that they just tore up your mortgage—the house is yours, free and clear! Picture the freedom that servant felt, the weight lifted off his shoulders!

That, in a nutshell, is forgiveness: setting offenders free of ever owing you anything in return for their offense against you. No revenge. No holding it over their head. No talking about them behind their backs. No expecting them to give you favors. The debt is canceled and gone. And when the ugly feelings rise up again within you, you refuse to give in to them. The debt is gone! Seventy times seven, the debt is gone! After all, that's what our Heavenly Father has done for us.

Living It Out

Vince D'Acchioli's wife, Cindy, taught him about forgiveness. In those days he was in top management with a Fortune 500 company, a Christian, but not living as one. Then came the day Cindy uncovered the secrets in his life that he had struggled to keep hidden. He pleaded with her, said he'd do whatever it took to salvage their relationship, even agreed to see a Christian counselor.

"Vince, I want you to look into your wife's eyes," the counselor said. After an uncomfortable amount of time, the counselor continued. "It has been said that you can tell the character of a man by looking into the eyes of his wife. I don't see much life in there, do you?" That cut Vince to the core. Vince would later learn that the forgiveness Cindy extended that day was in response to God's whisper, "If you will forgive Vince, I promise you there will be a third-day resurrection."

Today, Vince heads On Target Ministries and has a special place in his heart for helping men to understand that God knows them and created them for a unique purpose, He's gifted them for that purpose, and He wants them to find His purpose. If it weren't for Cindy's forgiveness, Vince might still be groping in the dark to grasp this himself.

———◆·••◆———

→ To what extent has God forgiven you of your missteps?

_____

_____

_____

_____

→ To what extent do you "pay it forward" and forgive as you've been forgiven?

_____

_____

_____

_____

→ Is there a person in your life you need to forgive? What a testimony that could be of the God who is known for such amazing grace if you were to go to that person and be reconciled!

_____

_____

_____

_____

Takeaway Truth

God is love. The very essence of love is giving of oneself unconditionally, no strings attached. Forgiveness is an expression of love that our Heavenly Father gives us and expects us to pass along to others. Nobody said it was easy. Imagine Jesus on the cross asking the Father to forgive His executioners, or Stephen saying the same thing of those who were stoning him to death (Acts 7:60)! Indeed, it takes strength only God can give. Now go and live today like Jesus and Stephen and so many others through the ages, releasing those who have wronged you with the gracious words, "I forgive you."

Valor Prayer

HOLY LORD, how vast is Your forgiveness to me! Because I am forgiven an infinite debt, I give up my right to revenge. I give up my right to "pay back." Like Peter and the disciples I say, "Lord, increase my faith!" I ask You to make me a merciful, forgiving man.

For Further Investigation

→ Matthew 6:9-15
→ Acts 7:54-60
→ Ephesians 4:32

Servanthood
Ready, Willing, Able

*"It ill becomes the servant to seek to be rich,
and great, and honored in that world where his Lord
was poor, and mean, and despised."*
—George Müeller

Read & Reflect

Read and reflect on Mark 10:35-45. Consider the following question: *What should be a man's attitude toward other people and their needs as he seeks to follow Jesus?*

_____

_____

_____

_____

The Challenge

James and John obviously knew all about "looking out for number one" before anyone ever coined the phrase. Jesus had just revealed to His first followers that He was going to be crucified and rise again, and they wanted to get first dibs on the best seats in His glory . . . or was it their own glory they wanted? After all, hadn't they successfully run a fishing business? Hadn't they been two of the three that had seen Jesus in His glory on the mountain (Mark 9:2-8)? They were natural choices for the favored positions when Jesus assumed His throne.

But Jesus put a God-sized pin in their self-serving bubble. The world's way is not God's way. "Looking out for number one" has no place in the kingdom of God. Jesus reminded them that they had no idea of the cost of their demands. While greatness in the eyes of the world means power and authority over others, Jesus said that's not the way to greatness for His followers. Jesus' way is much more difficult and self-denying. His way is the way of a servant.

Greatness in God's kingdom comes from being a humble servant, a "slave of all." Just a few days after this discussion, Jesus demonstrated what He meant (see John 13). As the Twelve came into the upper room to eat the Last Supper, Jesus washed their feet. He was the only man in the universe who could claim His own glory, yet Jesus laid it aside to clean the dusty, sweaty feet of His disciples. Because Jesus "did not come to be served, but to serve, and to give his life as a ransom for many" (Mark 10:45), God highly exalted Him. The more we serve others, the more we become like Jesus.

Living It Out

The birth of William Booth in Nottingham, England, in 1829 would lead to the birth of an organization serving society's outcasts—alcoholics, prostitutes, criminals and the like—that is still going strong today.

Born into a home of modest means, William's family descended into poverty with his dad's bad investments. Rather than being torn apart, they grew closer to each other and deeper with God. Later, it prompted 15-year-old William to leave a promising career as a pawnbroker to become a street preacher. And when he and Catherine were married, it spurred the young couple to open soup kitchens and homes for the destitute—an outreach that later became The Salvation Army.

William believed that an "army" of servant soldiers was needed to fight what plagued society. Within two decades there were a thousand British Salvation Army Corps, with many more dispatched to other continents. Before his death in 1912, William saw the army advance in 58 countries and colonies. Today, more than 2 million soldiers continue the work in 111 nations.

"My only hope for the permanent deliverance of mankind from misery, either in this world or the next," William added in his 1890 bestseller *In Darkest England and the Way Out,* "is the regeneration or remaking of the individual by the power of the Holy Spirit through Jesus Christ." So toward that end he strove, ever extending a cup of cold water in Jesus' name, ever enlisting fresh recruits into the army of God.

→ What comes more naturally, "looking out for number one" or helping others in need? Why do you think that's the case?

_____

_____

_____

_____

→ How would you describe the way of the servant? Who in your life is an ideal example of this?

_____

_____

_____

_____

→ How might God use a man like you—and men in your circle of influence—to serve in the spirit of William Booth today?

_____

_____

Takeaway Truth

God humbled Himself to serve us. The King of the universe left His throne to dwell among us. In the ultimate act of servanthood, Christ Jesus willingly went to the cross. Think about it. This should give you a new perspective on serving others! And yet, here we are with opportunities all around us to put others' needs above our own and to offer a helping hand. Imagine the impact you could have by serving others in Jesus' name. What might that look like in your world? How might that play out? Now go and live today as a servant of the Lord, providing hope to the helpless in a lost and hurting world!

Valor Prayer

FATHER GOD, Great Shepherd of the Sheep, thank You that You sent Your Son into the world not to be served but to serve, and to give His life as a ransom for many (Matthew 20:28). That is how I came to be a servant in Your army. Forgive me for all the times I sought to look out for number one and neglected the cries of others. May I have eyes to see and not ignore the physical and spiritual needs of those around me. So many needs, so little time. May I hear from You, my Commanding Officer, to know which need is a personal call for me to meet . . . in Jesus' name.

For Further Investigation

→ 1 Corinthians 9:19-23
→ Galatians 5:13-14
→ Philippians 2:3-7

Witness
Proclaiming Good News

*"Each generation of the church in each setting
has the responsibility of communicating the gospel in
understandable terms, considering the language
and thought-forms of that setting.*
—Francis Schaeffer

Read & Reflect
Read and reflect on John 1:35-51. Consider the following question: *Who in my world needs to know about Jesus, and am I ready, willing, and able to be His ambassador?*

_____

_____

_____

_____

The Challenge
Never had Andrew and Philip met such a man! Andrew's rabbi, John the Baptist, called Jesus the Lamb of God, the Messiah who would take away the sins of the world. Philip was simply overcome by the very presence of Jesus. So when Jesus spoke the simple command, "Follow me," the two men left everything and went after Jesus. But they could not contain their wonder at meeting the Christ, the one whose arrival God's people anticipated because God had promised it in their Scriptures.

Overcome with joy, both men looked for opportunities to tell others about their new Master. Andrew went immediately to his brother Peter and took him to Jesus. Philip found his friend Nathanael, excitedly spoke about finding the Messiah, and then took his buddy to meet Jesus. No great sermons. No theological expositions. They simply took those they loved to meet the one who could offer forgiveness and life everlasting.

Andrew and Philip were not scribes, priests, or Pharisees who were learned in the Law of Moses. They were ordinary men. Andrew was a fisherman. Philip was a guy Jesus met in Galilee who happened to be from the same town as Andrew. But each time they appear in the Gospels, they are following Jesus and taking others to meet Him (see John 12:20-22). In fact, once they knew that He was the promised Savior, they brought everyone they could to meet Him. By the power of the Holy Spirit who lives within, God uses modern-day Christ followers to be His witnesses in much the same way today (Acts 1:8)!

Living It Out

Have you heard of *The Four Spiritual Laws*? It's a little pamphlet that features a four-point plan that clearly explains the Good News of Jesus Christ. More than 100 million copies in every major language have been given out worldwide. Starting off with the simple promise of God's love and wonderful plan for a person's life, it's one of the most effective tools to tell others about Jesus (see 4laws.com). Bill Bright, the man who penned it, did so to help others find the life-changing truth he had found.

Born in Oklahoma in 1921, Bill grew up in a comfortable home. He was quite satisfied to dream dreams, build businesses, make money, and enjoy life. He was a self-proclaimed "happy pagan" who had no need for God. That changed when he headed west to launch Bright's California Confections. One day he stepped into Hollywood Presbyterian Church, where God convicted him of his sin and convinced him of his need for a Savior, Jesus Christ.

So moved by the Good News of God's grace, Bill wanted the world to know! His mission, a personal call from God, was to present the claims of Christ "to every living person on earth." What began as an unassuming campus ministry at nearby UCLA became an expansive outreach called Campus Crusade for Christ—or *Cru*—now based in Orlando, Florida, with some 30,000 full-time employees serving in nearly 200 countries.

What was the secret to such a vibrant ministry that flourishes today, long after Bill's passing in 2003? "When I was a young man I made a contract with God," Bill once said. "I literally wrote it out and signed my name at the bottom. It said, 'From this day forward, I am a slave of Jesus Christ.'" The apostle Paul once said, "Follow my example, as I follow the example of Christ" (1 Corinthians 11:1). How might the Gospel advance if we followed such examples of God-fearing men?

＊＊＊

✦ How did you first learn about the Good News of Jesus Christ?

_____

_____

_____

_____

✦ Who would make the list of those in your life who need to hear about Jesus?

_____

_____

_____

_____

_____

➔ Jesus said that His followers would be filled with the Holy Spirit and serve as His witnesses (Acts 1:8). What's preventing you from being ready, willing, and able to be a modern-day Bill Bright?

_____

_____

_____

_____

Takeaway Truth

God's plans are perfect. It might not seem like the best approach, entrusting the precious message of salvation to imperfect people like us, but that is precisely God's plan. Who better to share the Good News of forgiveness than broken men and women who have been redeemed? You have a story to tell that others will identify with because it's real. When in doubt, follow the apostles' example when they said: "For we cannot help speaking about what we have seen and heard" (Acts 4:20). Now go and live today proclaiming God's amazing story of forgiveness and redemption and invitation!

Valor Prayer

HEAVENLY FATHER, I recall how Jesus' eyes filled with tears when He traveled from place to place and had pity upon the helpless, hopeless, hurting, and lost—men, women, and children destined for an eternity apart from You if nothing changed (Matthew 9:35-38). Oh, Lord, break my heart with what breaks Yours! Help me to be obedient to You, to yield to the Spirit's power and be guided by the Spirit to share the Gospel with those around me. Here's a dangerous prayer: Like Bill Bright, from this day forward, I am a slave of Jesus Christ.

For Further Investigation

➔ Romans 1:16
➔ 1 Corinthians 15:1-11
➔ 2 Corinthians 5:16-21

Endurance
Running All Out

*"No one can sum up all that God is
able to accomplish through one solitary life,
wholly yielded, adjusted, and obedient to Him."*
—Henry Blackaby

Read & Reflect

Read and reflect on Hebrews 11:1-12:3. Consider the following question: *In light of all the forces against Christians in our world, how can I finish well as I follow Jesus?*

_____

_____

_____

_____

The Challenge

How do you encourage people to "hang in there!" when they've been forced to flee their homes and livelihoods because of their faith? These Hebrew Christians had already endured severe persecution years before, and now the nightmare had returned. They were discouraged, doubtful, and some even considered deserting their faith. *Where is God when all this is happening? How can He let my family go through this?* Over and over in the book of Hebrews, the writer encourages God's people to persevere, endure, and stay the course even in the face of gut-wrenching pain.

You see, the author of Hebrews knew some truths that give us hope in the midst of life's hardships, truths that emerge from the examples of faithful forefathers—people our faithful God had carried to the end. There's Abraham, Jacob, Moses, and a host of other weak, wounded men not unlike us who made it to the end because God is faithful. Since God empowered them to endure, wouldn't He do the same for us?

Of course, to endure over the long haul we have to "lighten the load." Not only do we need to resist sin, but we also need to eliminate anything in our lives that distracts us from Jesus, because He is the One who takes us all the way to the finish line. We need to focus exclusively on Jesus and His priorities.

Just like the rest of the New Testament, Hebrews is all about Jesus. He is superior to all the angels, greater than Moses and the rest of the prophets; He is the unique Son of God. He is the One who got us started in this race and He is the One who will perfect us as we run. He is the goal of our race and—with our eyes fixed on Him—we can hang in there until the end no matter what life throws at us!

Living It Out

"Don't let others create your world for you, for they will always create it too small." So said Edwin Louis Cole, or simply "Ed" to the countless men he ministered to in the mid to late twentieth century. Ed is commonly known as "the father of the Christian men's movement." His life is an apt illustration of what God can do in and through a man who is committed to Him.

Ed was born in Dallas and raised by a devout Christian mother. At the age of four, the family moved from Dallas to Los Angeles when a doctor prescribed sea air and sun to heal Ed's severe case of scarlet fever. There he grew up around Angelus Temple, where he played trumpet with the church's Skid Row witnessing team.

Though his faith faltered while serving in World War II, he and his new bride became fully devoted Christ-followers after the war. From street preacher to pastor, missions work to TV ministry, the next several decades were filled with sold-out service to the Lord. Then in the early 1980s, God impressed on him that "men were wasting themselves in selfish pursuits rather than pursuing the things of God," and that he'd been called to drop everything in favor of ministry to men.

So Ed held rallies, organized conferences, and wrote such books as *Maximized Manhood*. He tirelessly carried out his mission to declare a standard for manhood, that "manhood and Christlikeness are synonymous." Up to his death in 2002, Ed prepared other men to continue the work. He never imagined the enduring impact his ministry would have. Indeed, if you've ever attended a men's conference, you are part of the legacy of Ed Cole.

———⊶⊷———

→ What are challenges Christian men through the years have had to face? Does a particular example come to mind?

_____

_____

_____

_____

→ What's the biggest challenge you face in your Christian life today?

_____

_____

_____

_____

→ Is there anything that is sapping your spiritual strength and keeping you from fully following Christ and enduring to the end? Will you do business with the Lord right now?

_____

_____

_____

_____

Takeaway Truth

God is not finished with you yet. As someone has said, "If you're not dead, you're not done!" That means if you are reading this, there are things left for you to complete here on earth. Where to get started? Remain in His Word. He speaks through it to guide people. And remain in prayer. Take some time each day and ask the Lord how you might fulfill your purpose in this generation. You're here for a reason, God isn't finished with you yet, and your best days are yet ahead of you. Now go and start each new day afresh, committing yourself to the role that He is inviting you to play in the building of His kingdom for the *gospel and generations!*

Valor Prayer

GRACIOUS GOD, I want to ensure there is nothing between You and me, that there are no barriers in our relationship because of me. May nothing keep me from fully following and serving You to the end. To do this, I pray in light of the psalmist's prayer: "Search me, O God, and know my heart; test me and know my anxious thoughts. See if there is any offensive way in me, and lead me in the way everlasting" (Psalm 139:23-24).

For Further Investigation

→ 1 Corinthians 9:24-27
→ Philippians 3:12-14
→ 2 Peter 1:3-15

Going Forward

Well done! You've finished a journey . . . But really, this journey is just beginning. Here's how you can keep in the right race at the right pace.

It is imperative that you continue the journey by meeting with God every day. This brings to mind the story of a particular Cambridge University student who was so determined to pray and read his Bible every morning that he rigged a contraption to help him get out of bed. The vibration of an alarm clock set fishing tackle in motion and the sheets, clipped to the line, moved into the air. Absolutely nothing would keep him from his standing morning meeting with the Lord!

If you need help getting a "quiet time" established in your life, consider the following outline for spending time with God from *Seven Minutes with God* (adapted here with permission from The Navigators). Bob Foster, the long-time Navigator who originally wrote this outline, said, "Do not become devoted to the habit, but to the Savior. Do it not because other men are doing it—not as a spiritless duty every morning, not merely as an end in itself, but because God has granted the priceless privilege of fellowship with Himself. Covenant with Him to guard, nourish, and maintain your morning watch of seven minutes."

How do you spend these seven minutes?

½ Minute

Invest the first 30 seconds preparing your heart. Thank God for the opportunities of this new day. You might pray, "Lord cleanse my heart so You can speak to me through the Scriptures. Open my heart. Fill my heart. Make my mind alert, my soul active, and my heart responsive. Surround me with Your presence during this time."

4 Minutes

Take the next four minutes to read the Bible. Your greatest need is to hear some word from God. Allow the Word to strike fire in your heart. Meet the Author!

2½ Minutes

After God has spoken through His Book, then speak to Him in prayer. One method is to incorporate four areas of prayer that you can remember with the word ACTS.

A—Adoration. This is the purest kind of prayer because it's all for God. Tell the Lord that you love Him. Reflect on His greatness.

C—Confession. Having seen Him, you now want to be sure every sin is cleansed and forsaken. "Confession" comes from a root word meaning "to agree together with." When we apply this to prayer, it means we agree with God's estimation of what we've done.

T—Thanksgiving. Think of several specific things to thank Him for: your family, your business, your church—even thank Him for hardships.

S—Supplication. This means to "ask for, earnestly and humbly." Ask for others, then ask for yourself. Include people around the world, missionaries, friends, and those who have yet to hear about Jesus.

It all adds up to seven minutes. "This is simply a guide," Bob emphasized. "Very soon you will discover that it is impossible to spend only seven minutes with the Lord. An amazing thing happens—seven minutes become 20, and it's not long before you're spending 30 precious minutes with Him."

We agree. Start with seven minutes a day, and see how the Lord leads. We know that He will, for connecting with men like you is why Jesus came in the first place!

Second, consider moving on to *Mighty Men of Valor: Book 2 – Courage* and *Mighty Men of Valor: Book 3 – Passion* in our series. The following suggestions are for men who opt not to continue on in the series as they have through this particular Bible study.

Third, if you've processed this study Side-by-Side or in a triad or small group setting, remember that Warrior Brothers continue to "be there" for one another. Commit to pray for and encourage one another. Pick up resources you feel would help your Warrior Brothers continue the Mighty Men of Valor journey. Keep the lines of communication open so you can catch up on others' lives, give updates on the progress you've made on issues that surfaced during this study, have an extended prayer time together.

Finally, look around and consider if there's a person or another group of men with whom you would like to process this material. As Solomon said, "Two are better than one" (Ecclesiastes 4:9); and as the writer of Hebrews added, "Let us not give up meeting together" (Hebrews 10:25). Never go it alone. Always have a Warrior Brother at your side, and always be there for the men in your sphere of influence.

The Lord is with you, Mighty Man of Valor! May He continue to bless and lead you.

About the Authors

Dean Ridings, Bob Jones, and Scott Ballenger serve with Make a Mark Ministries—see www.makeamark.net—and are actively involved in a variety of disciple-making and men's ministry initiatives.

Dean has an M.Div. and serves with Focus on the Family in Colorado Springs. He and his wife, Kim, have four children. Email Dean at dean@makeamark.net.

Bob has a Th.M. and teaches at Rampart High School in Colorado Springs. He and his wife, Kate, have three children. Email Bob at bob@makeamark.net

Scott, director of Make a Mark Ministry, has a BSCS and is a senior engineer at VMware. The father of two, Scott and his wife, Robin, also live in Colorado Springs. Email Scott at scott@makeamark.net.

For information on Make a Mark Ministries or other resources that we offer, find us online at www.makeamark.net.

A Make a Mark Ministries Bible Study Series
www.makeamark.net

Mighty Men of Valor have three distinct characteristics: Strength, Courage & Passion

Men need Strength that comes from God alone, the kind of strength He gave men like Gideon—who lived at a time when everyone did what was right in their own eyes—David and his band of mighty men, and Jesus' early church followers!

Men need Courage to stand strong in increasingly challenging times, because we live in a world that's not what God created—evil exists, and as someone has said, "All it takes for evil to flourish is good men to stand by and do nothing"!

Men need Passion to live in light of the fact that the God of the universe chose us to be His children, called us to be kingdom men, and enables us to passionately live like Jesus and advance His Gospel where we live, work, and play through the generations!

Go through the entire Mighty Men of Valor series!

1. Use these studies as a daily devotional. We strongly encourage every man to take time out for a daily meeting—or appointment—with God.
2. Work through these studies with another man. Think of this as walking "Side-by-Side," meeting weekly for mutual growth, support, and accountability.
3. Connect with other men in a triad or small-group setting. Think of Jesus, who invested in a small group of 12 men, guiding them on the spiritual journey.

MINISTRIES

To order titles in the Mighty Men of Valor series:
www.makeamark.net

Made in the USA
Charleston, SC
30 January 2013